RUMI'S

Little Book of the

HEART

MARYAM MAFI & AZIMA MELITA KOLIN

HAMPTON ROADS

Cover design by Jim Warner
Cover photograph Two Little Ink Birds, 2014, (ink on paper),
    Moniz Charalambous, Nancy / Private Collection / Bridge-
    man Images
Typeset in Sabon

Hampton Roads Publishing Company, Inc.
Charlottesville, VA 22906
Distributed by Red Wheel/Weiser, LLC
www.redwheelweiser.com

Sign up for our newsletter and special offers by going to
www.redwheelweiser.com/newsletter/.

ISBN: 978-1-57174-742-6
Library of Congress Control Number: 2016933568

Printed in the United States of America
FR
10 9 8 7 6 5 4 3 2

Contents

Introduction

I t is the thirteenth century and times are tumultuous in the East. The Persian Empire is in chaos and division and corruption are rife amongst the ruling classes. The Mogul armies of Genghis Khan are moving westward, invading and pillaging country after country. People are living in fear and disbelief, having lost faith in their political and religious leaders. The Persians will soon bear witness to one of the worst massacres in history at the hands of the Mogul invaders.

Mowlana Jallaledin Mohamad Rumi is born on 30 September 1207, on the far eastern edge of the Persian Empire in Balkh in modern-day Afghanistan. His father, Baha-e Valad, is a renowned religious leader with a great following. A descendant of a long line of theologians, teachers, scholars and Islamic jurists, he eventually falls into disfavor with the brutal local ruler. Fearing

N.B. The calligraphy opposite represents Rumi's name.

the impending Mogul invasion, Rumi's father gathers his family and followers and leaves his homeland. After years of traveling during the mayhem of war and destruction they eventually arrive in Konya, in the province of Rum in present-day Turkey. Konya, melting pot of many cultures, religions and nationalities, is also a center of science, literature and learning. Rumi, now in his teens, is nourished in an atmosphere of love, stability and intellectual richness. Meanwhile the Turkish leader of the province offers Baha-e Valad his own school and the family settles permanently in Konya. Years later, after his father's death, the young erudite Rumi assumes the teaching post in the same school, not only leading his father's students but gaining thousands more on his own merit.

In 1244 Rumi, now thirty-six and an established scholar and religious leader, encounters Shams of Tabriz, a man in his sixties who is to shake the very foundations of Rumi's life. Shams' background is unclear, his appearance is shabby and his manner is rough and uncompromising. A *dervish,* or wandering mystic, Shams is a highly advanced *Sufi* walking the spiritual path of Love. Rumi recognizes in Shams a great master and, from their first encounter, becomes devoted to him. The meeting of these two men is like the meeting of two mighty rivers. Highly accomplished spiritual beings, each man recognizes in the other the confidant he has been seeking. Shams, searching all his life for someone who can truly understand him and receive his knowledge, finally finds that person in Rumi. They spend hours secluded from others immersed in meditation and spiritual talk. Shams encourages Rumi to resign from teaching, discard all his beloved books and refuse to see any of his students and followers. Instead he takes him on the path to the Love of God through insight, music, dance, and ultimately, poetry. This of course raises many eyebrows, and jealousies erupt among Rumi's dedicated followers. They regard Shams as a scruffy old man unworthy of the company of their master and who has distanced him from them. Eventually their petty behavior leaves Shams no option but to abandon the side of his adored friend without leaving a trace.

Hearing the news Rumi goes into deep seclusion and refuses to see anyone. The pain of separation from his beloved friend provokes him to begin expressing his longing and his suffering in poetry for the first time. His devotees eventually become exasperated and admit that it is better to have Shams back than never to see Rumi again. After months of searching Rumi finally receives a letter from Shams who is now in Damascus. Rumi sends his older son, Sultan Valad, and many followers to implore Shams to come back to Konya. The moment Rumi sees Shams' face again he regains his composure. They resume their discourse and immerse themselves in music and *sema,* a whirling spiritual dance. For a while Shams and Rumi are spared from the jealous eyes of the devotees. Rumi even manages to convince Shams to marry a young girl named Kimia, who is a member of Rumi's household. Shams indeed falls in love with Kimia but it is not meant to be. Only a year later Kimia dies following sudden illness. Overwhelmed with grief, and his discontent with the behavior of people around Rumi, Shams disappears again—this time for good.

There are different versions of what happens to Shams. Some say Rumi's followers, assisted by his younger son Allaedin, murder Shams and toss his body down a well. Others say Shams had realized the time for him to go had arrived and that if he stayed he would only curtail Rumi's spiritual growth. No one can be certain. Perhaps it really does not matter. The truth is that Shams appears in Rumi's life at the right moment and turns an educated, intelligent religious leader into an enlightened being. He shines in Rumi's life like the sun that he is, and disappears just as suddenly as he walked into it.

Rumi and Shams spend a total of two years together, after which Rumi becomes the great mystic poet we know today. Streams of poetry pour through his lips in praise of Shams, of Higher Truth and of Love. The agony of separation from his most beloved friend is overwhelming, as seen in his verse. Eventually, however, he realizes that the "friend" he is truly longing for is his own inner self, whom Shams had so clearly reflected. He becomes the sun that warms and transforms hearts, attracting people from all creeds, classes and religions.

His funeral in 1273 is attended by thousands of mourning Moslems, Christians, Jews, Greeks, Arabs, Persians and Turks. Rumi calls death a wedding with eternity, and his words reach us through seven centuries: "Do not weep over me . . . Do not say how sad . . . To you my death may seem a setting . . . But really it is a dawn."

What we have in our hands today of Rumi's journey, his struggles and his arrival is colossal volumes of teaching written in verse: the *Divan e Kabir* and the *Massnavi*. Rumi's *Rubaiyat,* the quatrains, consisting of 1659 verses, are much less known in the West. Many of the quatrains were set to music and sung in *Sufi* gatherings and *sema* performances. No one can precisely allocate them to specific periods of Rumi's life. Some were written while Shams was still with Rumi, others poured from his lips after Shams was gone. Like crystals, they sparkle with rainbow colors and contain worlds inside. As we hold them in our hands, they capture us with their mystery. Transparent and clear they open doors to the wonder of inner spaces and longing. Traced in Persian calligraphy, Rumi's words are like writings on water, dancing and embracing our souls. They are the whispers of two lovers in a crowd. Allow them to caress your ears and penetrate your heart. They will take you to places where your spirit will be at home.

This book is the fruit of a joyous meeting between two friends sharing their love for Rumi. At first, choosing and translating poems from the *Rubaiyat* was more an excuse to spend time together with Rumi and deepen our understanding of him. As time went on, we were faced with the challenge of finding words to unravel the hidden subtleties of his language. Like the different facets of a cut diamond, the poems revealed more layers of colors, angles and meaning every time we reread them. Dipping into the vast ocean of Rumi's works became an experience of great awe, discovery and joy. Sometimes we were uplifted, sometimes lost for words, but every time more enriched and more in love. It is in gratitude for these moments that we present these poems with the hope to share them with you.

Dear heart, where do you find
the courage to seek the Beloved
when you know He has annihilated
so many like you before?
I do not care, said my heart,
my only wish is to become
one with the Beloved.

First, he tempted me
with infinite caresses.
He burnt me in the end
with pain and sorrow.
In this game of chess
I had to lose myself
in order to win Him.

We are bound together.
I am the ground
You are the step.
How unfair is this Love!
I can see Your world
but You, I cannot.

I cannot sleep in your presence.
In your absence, tears prevent me.
You watch me My Beloved
on each sleepless night and
only You can see the difference.

Prayer clears the mist
and brings back peace to the soul.
Every morning, every evening
let the heart sing,
La ilaha il Allah.
"There is no reality but God."

Looking at my life
I see that only Love
has been my soul's companion.
From deep inside
my soul cries out:
Do not wait, surrender
for the sake of Love.

Are you searching for your soul?
Then come out of your prison.
Leave the stream and join the river
that flows into the ocean.
Absorbed in this world
you've made it your burden.
Rise above this world.
There is another vision . . .

Your charm lured me
to the edge of madness.
I lost my composure.
Humbled, I was sent away.
Then, You touched my heart,
transformed and shaped me
into any form You fancied.

All year round the lover is mad,
unkempt, lovesick and in disgrace.
Without love there is nothing but grief.
In love . . . what else matters?

If you can't smell the fragrance
don't come into the garden of Love.
If you're unwilling to undress
don't enter into the stream of Truth.
Stay where you are.
Don't come our way.

Love is our mother and
the way of our Prophet.
Yet, it is in our nature
to fight with Love.
We can't see you, mother,
hidden behind dark veils
woven by ourselves.

If you have illusions about heaven
lose them.
The soul heard of one attribute of Love
and came to earth.
A hundred attributes of heaven
could never charm her back.
It is here the soul discovers
the reality of Love.

When I die,
lay my corpse to rest,
but do not be at all surprised
if His kiss on my tattered lips
brings me back to life.

Sometimes I feel like a king,
sometimes I moan in my own prison.
Swaying between these states
I can't be proud of myself.
This "I" is a figment of my imagination.

I saw my Love walking on her own,
tall and slender, dreamy eyes,
with primroses in her hands.
I leapt to steal a kiss,
she cried:
"Help, help, thief!"

Imitating others,
I failed to find myself.
I looked inside and discovered
I only knew my name.
When I stepped outside
I found my real Self.

Do you want to enter paradise?
To walk the path of Truth
you need the grace of God.
We all face death in the end.
But on the way, be careful
never to hurt a human heart!

Do you know what the music is saying?
"Come follow me and you will
find the way.
Your mistakes can also lead you
to the Truth.
When you ask, the answer
will be given."

I am happy tonight,
united with the Friend.
Free from the pain of separation,
I whirl and dance with the Beloved.
I tell my heart, "Do not worry,
the key to morning I've thrown away."

The Master who's full of sweetness
is so drunk with love, he's oblivious.
"Will you give me
some of your sweetness?"
"I have none," he says,
unaware of his richness.

Peaceful
is the one
who's not concerned
with having more or less.
Unbound by name and fame
he is free from sorrow
from the world and
mostly from
himself.

The one who cuts off your head
is your friend.
The one who puts it back
is a deceiver.
The one who weighs you
with his troubles
is your burden.
But the one who truly loves you
will set you free.

You know what love is?
It is all kindness, generosity.
Disharmony prevails when
you confuse lust with love, while
the distance between the two
is endless.

Deafened by the voice of desire
you are unaware the Beloved
lives in the core of your heart.
Stop the noise,
and you will hear His voice
in the silence.

Invoking Your name
does not help me to see You.
I'm blinded by the light of Your face.
Longing for your lips
does not bring them any closer.
What veils You from me
is my memory of You.

There is a way from your heart to mine
and my heart knows it,
because it is clean and pure like water.
When the water is still like a mirror
it can behold the Moon.

Reason, when you speak
I cannot hear the Wise One.
Even if you are as thin as a hair
still there's no space for you.
In the flaming Sun
all bright lights are put to shame.

This Love is a King
but his banner is hidden.
The Koran speaks the Truth
but its miracle is concealed.
Love has pierced with its arrow
the heart of every lover.
Blood flows but the wound is invisible.

Why is my heart so troubled?
Why has love reduced me to nothing?
Why does this heart of mine
fight with me day and night?
Why?

Who are you complaining to?
I asked the reed,
Why do you moan and grieve?
"Since they've cut me from the riverbed,
what else is left for me
but to weep?"

I said to the night,
"If you are in love with the moon,
it is because you never stay for long."
The night turned to me and said,
"It is not my fault. I never see the Sun,
how can I know that love is endless?"

To be or not to be
is not my dilemma.
To break away from both worlds
is not bravery.
To be unaware of the wonders
that exist in me,
that
is real madness!

Holding on to your feet
I cannot reach your hands.
Who can I turn to,
when it's only Your Love I want?
You tease me, saying,
"I see no tears in your eyes."
My heart is broken, can't you see
the drops on my eyelashes?

O Friend,
You made me lovingly,
put me in a dress of skin and blood.
Then planted deep inside me
a seed from Your heart.
You turned the whole world
into a sanctuary where You are
the only One.

I asked for a kiss,
You gave me six.
From whom did You learn
such mastery?
Full of kindness, generosity . . .
You are not of this world.

When I touch the ground in prayer
I have no other purpose
but You.
All else I speak about
gardens, flowers, nightingales, whirling
is only an excuse.

I'm pleased with my sight
when I behold the Friend.
But my vision and the Friend
cannot be two.
It is He, who sees with my eyes.

I was talking about You,
You silenced me.
I tasted your sweetness
and everything stopped.
Bewildered, I fled to
the house of my heart
and there,
you caught me.

Heat is not brought by fire only.
When you suddenly walk
through my door, I feel warm.
When you promise to come but do not
I feel desolate and cold.
Frost does not appear in winter only.

Be thirsty heart,
seek forever without a rest.
Let *this* soundless longing
hidden deep inside you
be the source
of every word you say.

Dreamy and distracted,
you stumbled upon the Friend.
You felt His presence
and froze on your path.
If you don't have
the strength to face Him,
why seek the circle of the Drunks?

You who only see me
as a pious man,
listen to what I have to say.
I have my faith but
I also have the world.
Poor are the ones
who have neither.

My Friend,
I offer You my life.
Accept me, make me drunk
and save me from both worlds.
Set me on fire
if my heart settles on anything
but You.

There is no wine without You.
No use for the rosary without Your hand.
From afar you order me to dance.
But unless you set the stage and
draw the curtain, my Beloved,
how can I dance?

You are the light of my heart
and the comfort of my soul.
You are a troublemaker too.
You keep asking,
"Have you seen The Friend?"
When you know so well that
The Friend can not be seen.

It's good to leave each day behind,
like flowing water, free of sadness.
Yesterday is gone and its tale told.
　　Today new seeds are growing.

Today I am so upset!
What I was hiding deep inside
You brought out in the light.
Overcome by sleep last night
You had caught me,
unaware.

I lay in the dust at Your feet,
my heart entangled
in the curls of Your hair.
I've had enough.
Bring closer Your lips
and let Your kiss
release my soul.

Lovers drink wine all day and night
and tear the veils of the mind.
When drunk with love's wine
body, heart and soul
become one.

Last night my Beloved
was like the moon, so beautiful!
He was even brighter than the Sun.
His grace is far beyond my grasp.
The rest is silence.

Be certain
in the religion of Love
there are no
believers or unbelievers.
Love embraces all.

Walking on Your path
he who dies to himself
will come to life.
You say:
"Don't get drunk and lose yourself."
But tell me,
how can one remain sober
drinking Your wine?

Beyond a hundred steps of wisdom,
I will be free from *good and bad*.
Behind the veils I will find
such Splendor, such Beauty
that I will fall in love
with Myself.

The early breeze at dawn
is the keeper of secrets.
Don't go back to sleep!
It is time for prayer,
time to find what
is your real need.
Don't go back to sleep!
The door of the One
is open, always.
Don't go back to sleep!

Dear heart, you are so unreasonable!
First you fall in love
then worry about your life.
You rob and steal
then worry about the law.
You profess to be in love
and still worry about what people say.

The heart is like a candle
longing to be lit.
Torn from The Beloved
it yearns to be whole again,
but you have to bear the pain.
You cannot learn about love.
Love appears on the wings of grace.

Last night
I begged the Wise One to tell me
the secret of the world.
Gently, gently he whispered,
"Be quiet,
the secret cannot be spoken,
it is wrapped in silence."

On my heart
in beautiful calligraphy
You've written words
that only You and I can know.
Their secret You promised
to reveal one day
but now I see
You were only teasing.

Love is the alchemy of the East.
Like the clouds it is pregnant
with a thousand bolts of lightning.
Deep within me
moves the ocean of his Splendor
and all creation springs from it.

My heart is so small
it's almost invisible.
How can You place
such big sorrows in it?
"Look," He answered,
"your eyes are even smaller,
yet they behold the world."

When you see the lovers
don't pass them by,
sit with them.
The fire of Love warms the world,
but even fire dies
in the company of ashes.

Whisper to me intimately like a lover,
for tenderness is rare in this world.
It is difficult to convey the magic of love
to those who are made of dust.

Walking in the garden with my lover,
I was distracted by a rose.
My love scolded me, saying
"How could you look at a rose
with my face so close?"

With friends you grow wings.
Alone
you are a single feather in disgrace.
With them you master the wind,
but alone,
you're blown in all directions.

Today is such a happy day.
There is no room for sadness.
Today we drink the wine of trust
from the cup of knowledge.
We can't live on bread and water alone.
Let us eat a little from the hand of God.

From all that was familiar,
I broke away.
Now I am lost, without a place,
wandering.
With no music like a fool
I dance and clap my hands.
How am I to live without You?
You are everywhere
but I can't find You.

Come, come
do you hear the music?
The *sema* has begun!
"Go away, I'm ill," I said.
"Oh, stop complaining,"
he pulled my ear.
"Come and see how
both worlds are dancing!"

A *dervish* gives freely
the secrets of the world.
His words, a precious gift.
He does not expect
his daily bread for free.
He gives his life and
asks for nothing in return.

I want a kiss from You,
said my heart.
"Yes, but the price
is your life."
My heart leaped with joy
and said,
Who cares about the price!

He is gone!

The one without a rival.

He is gone!

The one I am never tired of.

No cure

for my broken heart.

The rose has lost its petals,

but the thorn is left behind.

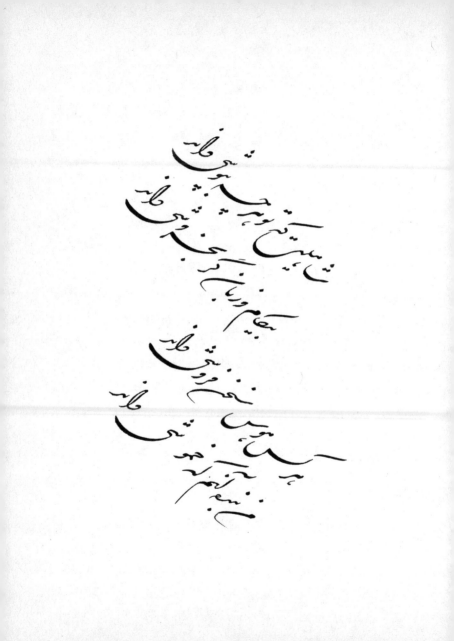

God knows you under any cover
He hears your unspoken words.
Everyone is tempted
by the eloquence of speech,
but I am the slave of
the master of silence.

Drowned in my sorrow,
why do you torment me too?
Bent to the ground by the world,
why do you kick me too?
I received my life from you,
tell me, do you want it back?

I asked,
"What about my eyes?"
I will fill them with tears.
I asked,
"What about my heart?"
I will break it with sorrow.
I asked,
"What about my body?"
I will crush and throw it away.

With love you don't bargain
there, the choice is not yours.
Love is a mirror, it reflects
only your essence,
if you have the courage
to look in its face.

To place You in my heart
may turn You into thought.
I will not do that!
To hold You with my eyes
may turn You into thorn.
I will not do that!
I will set You on my breath
so You will become my life.

When you fast for a while
your nature is cleansed.
With the pure-of-heart
you may enter the garden.
To become light,
fast and burn like a candle.
Each morsel is the link that
chains you to the ground.

Awakened by your love,
I flicker like a candle's light
trying to hold on in the dark.
Yet, you spare me no blows
and keep asking,
"Why do you complain?"

Laying a myriad of traps,
you are so cunning, my Love.
Even if the world
turns into one big stone,
I wouldn't be surprised
to see your windmill
grind it into dust.

You opened the door of my heart
and filled it with the pain of love.
Shaken, I ran to seek comfort
from others, but they
did not respond to my lament.
Alone and desperate, I beg You,
do not forsake me now.

You are so near
that I cannot see You.
Like a fool I keep looking around.
Your hand cannot reach me,
I'm wrapped in so many veils
My heart sobs, inconsolable . . .

Be honest dear heart,
broken and abashed,
how can you still chase love?
Without a drop of water
how dare you enter
the raging fire of love?
Tell me foolish heart,
what can I do with you?

You are the cure hidden in the pain.
Concealed in anger and betrayal
is Your compassion and loyalty.
You are not only in heaven,
I see Your footprints
everywhere on earth.

For years I kept calling You.
Then suddenly, You came at dawn
and whirled me to the *sema*.
You left me with not a moment to spare,
even for my morning prayer.

When compassion fills my heart,
free from all desire,
I sit quietly like the earth.
My silent cry echoes like thunder
throughout the universe.

Be motivated like the falcon,
hunt gloriously.
Be magnificent as the leopard,
fight to win.
Spend less time with
nightingales and peacocks.
One is all talk,
the other only color.

The time has come to turn your heart
into a temple of fire.
Your essence is gold hidden in dust.
To reveal its splendor
you need to burn in the fire of love.

What pure perfection Love is,
pure perfection!
What an illusion our ego is,
what an illusion!
This love is a glory,
what Glory!
Today is the day of union,
the day of our union.

This world is full of men like Jesus,
not a place for doubt and sorrow.
Why allow salt water to rust your heart,
when the world is brimming
with pure sweet water.

I'm stubborn, ecstatic and nosy;
my friend so delicate,
impatient and weary.
Without a messenger between us
how can we find harmony?
We can only meet
in God's presence.

There are no signposts in the desert,
caravans are guided by the stars.
In the darkness of despair
hope is the only light.
But in the garden of your life,
my dear, never hope that
a weeping willow will give you dates.

The birds have flown to freedom,
the cage lies empty.
Your happy songs bring to me
the scent of heaven.
Please keep singing.

I was nothing,
you made me greater
than a mountain.
I lagged behind,
you pushed me to the front.
My heart was shattered,
you healed it.
I turned into a lover
of Myself.

Where have you gone my love?
You left me broken, hopeless.
I will mourn for you as long as I live.
Hope comes in hopelessness.

There was once a clever, cunning man
sitting comfortably on his horse.
For God he did not care,
nor for the world or truth or faith.
Tell me, how can such a man
respect this world or the next?

I want to be free
from this ego dog of mine.
I tie a collar of repentance
around his neck,
but once he sniffs the scent of blood
he tears it to pieces.
How can I tame this mad dog of mine?

I was delighted with myself,
having offered everything I had;
my heart, my faith, my work.
"And who are you," you said,
"to think you have so much to offer?
It seems you have forgotten
where you've come from."

I tried to give You up and
live without the pain of longing.
I tried to be empty of all passion for
You.
I failed.
Now, I know my master,
had I been a real man
I should've never tried.

I hoped my grief to be my cure,
but I drowned in helplessness.
You asked me out of kindness,
"What is your wish?"
"What I want is You," I answered.
"That, I cannot promise."

On my quest
I feel so confused and restless.
Set on fire, my heart explodes
with the pain of separation.
In this struggle, I am caught forever
unless I go beyond this
You and *I*.

I've given up work and
forsaken my livelihood.
Instead I write poetry.
My sight, my heart, my life
belong to Him.
All three words
I have woven into one,
LOVE.

Terms and Symbolism

Beloved, Friend, Lover, King
God in His loving aspect
The lover
The Sufi in search of the Beloved
Burning
The process of purification of the soul
Darvish, Dervish
Sufi mystic
Drunk, drunkenness
Intoxication with the love of God
Reed
Longing for return to the source
Killing
Breaking one's attachment to the ego
Nightingale
Symbol of the soul's longing
Ocean
The limitless universe of God
Rose
Symbol of the beauty of the Beloved
Rose-garden
Paradise and eternal beauty
Sema, Sama
Spiritual whirling dance of the darvishes
Sufi
Mystic in search of the Beloved
Wine
Symbol of the ecstasy of the love of God

Acknowledgments

Calligraphy by Hassan Behrast Shayjani
Art work of emblem by Nuran Gungorencan

Our heartfelt thanks to Charlie Gore, Bertrand Fritsch, Diane McCree, Mr Bordbar, LMSR Nezam Mafi, Nigel Watts, Moray Welsh and all our friends who unlocked doors for us at the most crucial moments.

Source Note

The translations were done from Badi-o Zaman Forouzanfar's edition of *The Divan*.

For those of you who wish to read more of the quatrains from the *Rubaiyat* of Mowlana Jallaledin Mohamad Rumi, their original numbering sequence is given below:

Page	*Quatrain*
p.9	No. 24
p.10	No. 14
p.11	No. 25
p.12	No. 36
p.13	No. 11
p.15	No. 42
p.16	No. 62
p.17	No. 48
p.18	No. 55
p.19	No. 60
p.21	No. 57
p.22	No. 61
p.23	No. 64
p.24	No. 67
p.25	No. 74
p.27	No. 77
p.28	No. 95
p.29	No. 99
p.30	No. 111

About the Editors

Maryam Mafi was born and raised in Iran and is an experienced Persian translator who has studied in the US and translated a variety of scholarly and poetic works. She lives in London.

Azima Melita Kolin was born in Bulgaria and is a concert pianist and an artist. She completed her studies at the musical academies in Sofia, Rome and Geneva and has won many international competitions in Germany, Italy, and Spain. She also studied painting and has had many exhibitions in the UK and abroad. She lives in London.

Hampton Roads Publishing Company
. . . for the evolving human spirit

Hampton Roads Publishing Company
publishes books on a variety of subjects,
including spirituality, health,
and other related topics.

For a copy of our latest trade catalog,
call (978) 465-0504
or visit our distributor's website at
www.redwheelweiser.com.

You can also sign up for our newsletter
and special offers by going to
www.redwheelweiser.com/newsletter/.